D1113681

GUIDE

VAN GOGH
MUSEUM

publisher
Van Gogh Museum, Amsterdam

distribution
Waanders Uitgevers, Zwolle

ISBN 90 400 9886 7
NUGI 921, 911

Contents

Foreword

Museums devoted to a single artist are
gradually becoming less of a rarity, and
one of the most prominent is the Van Gogh
Museum. Nowhere else in the world can
one get such a sweeping impression of
Vincent van Gogh's art as in Amsterdam.
In addition to enjoying world-famous
masterpieces from each period in the
artist's career, such as *The potato eaters,*
The bedroom, Sunflowers and *Wheatfield*
with crows, it is only here that visitors have
the opportunity of getting to know many
dozens of less well-known studies.
The Van Gogh Museum has even higher
ambitions. Its aim is to display Vincent van
Gogh surrounded by the art of his own day
– the second half of the 19th century. Van
Gogh's work hangs here in the company
of paintings by his friends Emile Bernard,
Henri de Toulouse-Lautrec and Paul
Gauguin. The museum also presents a
survey of the 19th-century art that preceded
and inspired Van Gogh, such as landscapes
from the School of Barbizon, and realistic
depictions of peasant life by Jean-François
Millet and Jules Breton. Finally, such
Impressionists as Claude Monet and
Symbolists like Odilon Redon can also be
admired here. The collection is regularly
enriched with new acquisitions.
We hope that this guide will help you in
your exploration of this unique museum,
and that as a souvenir it will provide you
with vivid memories of your visit.

Ronald de Leeuw

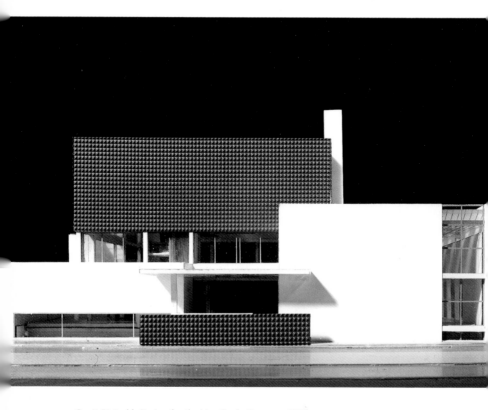

Gerrit Rietveld, Design for the Van Gogh Museum, 1963

Museum and collection

History

'And my aim in life is to make as many good pictures and drawings as I can, and as well as I can. Then, at the end of my life, I hope simply to pass away while looking back with love and wistfulness, thinking "Oh, the pictures I might have made!" But this, mind you, does not preclude doing what is possible.'

Vincent van Gogh 1883

The Van Gogh Museum, which opened in 1973, contains more than 200 paintings, 580 drawings, four sketchbooks and around 750 letters by Vincent van Gogh. The collection also includes works by Vincent's contemporaries which the artist and his brother Theo bought or acquired through exchanges. A few years ago the museum adopted a supplementary purchasing policy designed to enlarge this group and create a broader framework than simply that of Vincent van Gogh surrounded by his artist friends. The museum has evolved into an institution where, with Van Gogh at its core, attention is also focused on the visual arts in Europe in the second half of the 19th century, with works by leading French artists like Puvis de Chavannes, Léon Lhermitte and Odilon Redon.

History

The museum may be young but its collection has a long history. Van Gogh's works originally belonged to Theo van Gogh (1857–1891), Vincent's younger brother, who worked at the art gallery of Goupil & Co. (later Boussod, Valadon & Cie.) in Paris. From the

Johanna Bonger with her son and second husband in Amsterdam, c. 1905

very beginning of his career Vincent sent most of his works to Theo in exchange for the latter's moral and financial support.

After Theo's death in 1891 the collection passed to his widow, Johanna van Gogh-Bonger (1862–1925). She moved back to Holland, where she did everything in her power to promote Vincent's work. She was the moving force behind exhibitions and also began selling pictures from the collection. Her efforts were rewarded, and when Van Gogh had gained international recognition in the second decade of the 20th century she decided to preserve what remained of the original collection.

From 1920 she rarely sold any more works.

After Johanna's death in 1925 the collection was inherited by her son, Vincent Willem van Gogh (1890–1978). In 1930 he decided to loan the bulk of it to the Stedelijk Museum in Amsterdam. This loan was largely due to Van Gogh's wife, Josina van Gogh-Wibaut (1891-1933), who felt that it was a pity that the public was unable to enjoy the many paintings by Van Gogh in the family collection.

Vincent Willem van Gogh, popularly known as 'the Engineer' (he was a mechanical engineer by profession) was at first rather diffident about his uncle's artistic legacy. It was only after the Second World War that he became actively involved with the collection, organising numerous exhibitions at home and abroad. In the 1950s he decided that the time had come to secure the future of the collection. On the initiative of the Dutch state, which pledged to build a museum devoted to Van Gogh, he transferred the works he owned to the newly-formed Vincent van Gogh Foundation in 1962.

Gerrit Rietveld (1888–1964), an architect of the Stijl movement, produced the first sketches for the museum a year later. Construction began in 1969, and the museum was officially opened on 2 June 1973.

The collection, which the Vincent

Dr Vincent Willem van Gogh

van Gogh Foundation gave on permanent loan to the Dutch state, had found its permanent home. By the early 1990s, the museum was attracting so many visitors that it was decided to expand and totally renovate it. The new exhibition wing was designed by the Japanese architect Kisho Kurokawa (b. 1934) and opened in 1999.

Permanent collection

The museum's permanent collection is on display in the building designed by Gerrit Rietveld. This part of the museum has four storeys and a basement which houses the auditorium. The ground and third floors are hung a broad selection from the museum's holdings of 19th-century European painting and sculpture, supplemented with works by Vincent van Gogh. The first floor is devoted entirely to the presentation of Van Gogh's most important works. It contains a large selection of his paintings, which are exhibited in chronological order so that the visitor can follow the development of Van

The Van Gogh Museum, 1999

Gogh's oeuvre step by step -- from the early works and the peasants of Nuenen, through the experiments with colour and technique in Antwerp and Paris, culminating in the masterpieces created in Arles, Saint-Rémy and Auvers-sur-Oise.

Part of the second floor has been set aside as a study area. Computers, books, educational displays and open storage depots enable visitors to explore the lives and works of 19th-century artists in greater depth. This floor also houses the printroom, which is used for the regular rotating exhibitions of works on paper from various collections. Van Gogh's own drawings and letters are only occasionally put on display because of their fragility and sensitivity to light.

Exhibitions

The wing designed by Kisho Kurokawa is used solely for the temporary exhibitions that the museum organises. It is in the shape of an ellipse and is partly below ground. A semicircular corridor, two large galleries and a printroom provide space for exhibitions on various aspects of 19th-century art. The construction of the new wing was made possible by a donation from The Japan Foundation, which was acting on behalf of the Yasuda Fire & Marine Insurance Company, Ltd of Japan.

The 19-year-old Vincent van Gogh, 1873

Van Gogh

The story of a life

'I am a man of passions, capable of and subject to doing more or less foolish things which I sometimes tend to regret. Now and then I speak or act too hastily, when it would have been better to be more patient.'

Vincent van Gogh July 1880

Vincent van Gogh was born on 30 March 1853 in Zundert, a village in the southern province of North Brabant. He was the eldest son of the Reverend Theodorus van Gogh (1822–1885) and Anna Cornelia Carbentus (1819–1907). At the age of 16 he started work at the Hague gallery of the French art dealers, Goupil & Co., in which his uncle Vincent was a partner. His brother Theo, who was born on 1 May 1857, later worked for the same firm.

In 1873 Goupil's transferred Vincent to London. Two years later they moved him to Paris, where he lost all ambition to become an art dealer. He immersed himself in religion, threw out his modern, worldly books, and became 'daffy with piety,' in the words of his sister Elisabeth. He was dismissed from Goupil's at the beginning of 1876. Van Gogh then took a job as an assistant teacher in England, but disappointed by the lacks of prospects he returned to Holland at the end of the year. He now decided to follow in his father's footsteps and become a clergyman. Although disturbed by his fanaticism and odd behaviour, his parents agreed to pay for the private lessons he would need to gain a place at university.

Vincent aged 13

Vincent's brother Theo in 1889

The Goupil & Co. gallery in The Hague

This proved to be another false start. Van Gogh abandoned the lessons, and after a brief spell of training as an evangelist went to the Borinage mining region in the south of Belgium. His ministry among the miners led him to identify deeply with them and their families. In 1879, however, his appointment was not renewed, and his parents despaired, regarding him as a social misfit. In an unguarded moment his father even spoke of committing him to a mental asylum.

Nuenen

Future as an artist

Vincent, too, was at his wits' end, and after a long period of solitary soul-searching in the Borinage he resolved to become an artist. His earlier desire to help his fellow-man as an evangelist gradually developed into an urge, as he later wrote, to leave mankind 'some memento in the form of drawings or paintings – not made to please any particular movement, but to express a sincere human feeling.' His parents could not go along with

this latest change of course, and the
financial responsibility for Vincent
passed to his brother Theo, who was
now working in the Paris gallery of
Boussod,Valadon & Cie., the succes-
sors of Goupil & Co. It was because
of Theo's loyal support that Van Gogh
later came to regard his oeuvre as
the fruits of his brother's efforts on
his behalf.

Unsuspected talents

When Van Gogh decided to become an
artist, no one, not even he himself,
suspected that he had extraordinary
artistic gifts. He evolved remarkably
rapidly from an inept but impassioned
novice into a truly original master.
He eventually proved to have an
exceptional feel for bold, harmonious
colour effects, and an infallible knack
of choosing simple but memorable
compositions.

Rue Lepic, Paris, the street in which
the Van Gogh brothers lived

Initially Van Gogh lived at his parents'
home in Etten, North Brabant, where
he set himself the task of learning
how to draw. At the end of 1881 he
moved to The Hague, and there too
he concentrated mainly on drawing.
In late 1883, after a brief stay in the
wilds of the moorland province of
Drenthe, he went back to live with his
parents, who had moved to the village
of Nuenen, near Eindhoven. It was
here that he first began painting
regularly, modelling himself chiefly
on the French painter Jean-François
Millet (1814–1875), who had caused
a sensation throughout Europe with
his scenes of the harsh life of peasants.
After two years spent in the countryside of Brabant, Van Gogh left for
Antwerp at the end of 1885, where he

View of Saint-Rémy from the
asylum garden

studied briefly at the art academy. In
early 1886 he went to live with his
brother in Paris. There, at last, he was
confronted with the modern art of the
Impressionists and Post-Impressionists.
He discovered that the dark palette
he had developed back in Holland
was hopelessly out-of-date, and mas-
tered the modern style within two

years – a remarkable achievement.
At the beginning of 1888, now a
mature artist, Van Gogh went south
to Arles, in Provence, where he at
last began to feel confident about his
choice of career. He now set out to
make a personal contribution to
modern art with his daring colour
combinations. Towards the end of
the year, though, his optimism was
rudely shattered by the first signs of
his illness, a type of epilepsy that

The 'Yellow House' in Saint-Rémy

took the form of delusions and psychotic attacks. It was during one of those seizures that he cut off his left ear-lobe.

The Ravoux inn, the boarding house where Van Gogh spent the last months of his life

The final years

In April 1889 he went to nearby Saint-Rémy, where he entered the Saint-Paul-de-Mausole asylum as a voluntary patient. He left at the end of May 1890 and went north again, this time to the rustic village of Auvers-sur-Oise, near Paris. Although he now had a small but growing circle of admirers, Van Gogh had lost his original passion. 'I feel – a failure,' he wrote to his brother. 'That's it as far as I'm concerned – I feel that this is the destiny that I accept, that will never change.' On 27 July 1890 he shot himself in the chest. He died two days later. Theo, who had stored the bulk of Vincent's work in Paris, died six months later. His widow, Johanna van Gogh-Bonger (1862–1925), returned to Holland with the collection, and dedicated herself to getting her brother-in-law the recognition he deserved. In 1914, with his fame assured, she published the correspondence between the two brothers. From that moment on Van Gogh's oeuvre became inextricably interwoven with the story of his remarkable and tragic life.

The tombstones of Vincent and Theo in Auvers

John Peter Russell, Portrait of Vincent van Gogh, 1886

Van Gogh

Paintings and drawings

'And yet, I believe that even if I go on producing work in which people can point to mistakes, it will still have a certain vitality and *raison d'être* of its own that will overpower those errors – in the eyes of those who appreciate character and the spiritual conception of things.'

Vincent van Gogh 1885

Van Gogh's career as an artist lasted barely ten years, but in that brief time he produced around 1,100 drawings and almost 900 paintings. By far the most important and varied group of works from this vast oeuvre is in the Van Gogh Museum. The Netherlands has a second collection of some 90 paintings and almost 200 drawings by Van Gogh. It was formed by Hélène Kröller-Müller at the beginning of this century and can now be seen in the Kröller-Müller Museum in Otterlo. The remaining works are scattered all over the world. What makes the collection in the Van Gogh Museum so exceptional is that it contains representative works illustrating each period in the artist's career. These is a strong showing of paintings from the Nuenen period (1883–1885), and includes the key canvases produced there, like The potato eaters 22. Amsterdam also has most of the paintings made during Van Gogh's three-month stay in Antwerp – mainly portraits and cityscapes.

His transformation in Paris from a follower of the Barbizon painters to a true Impressionist can be traced step by step in the museum's 85 paintings from this period. They include an impressive series of 17 self-portraits. Masterpieces from Van Gogh's Arles period include The Yellow House ('The Street') 40, The bedroom 42, Sunflowers 45, and what is perhaps his most beautiful landscape, The harvest 38. The months that he spent in the asylum at Saint-Rémy are represented by The reaper 47, Vase of irises 51 and Almond blossom 48. From the last month of Van Gogh's life in Auvers-sur-Oise come spectacular canvases like Wheatfield under thunderclouds 54 and Wheatfield with crows 55, which was long thought to have been his last work.

Nuenen

On 4 December 1883 Van Gogh travelled from Drenthe, where he had been working for three months, to Nuenen – a village in the province of Brabant where his father had been pastor since 1882. Vincent had decided to return home, despite the fact that he did not get on very well with his parents. 'They feel the same dread of taking me into the house as they would about letting in a great shaggy dog. He'll come into the room with wet paws – and really, he is so shaggy. He'll get in everyone's way. And he's got such a loud bark. A foul beast, in short,' Vincent wrote to Theo.

In Brabant Van Gogh discovered weavers and peasants, and he also made many landscape drawings. Above all, though, he practised depicting the human figure, for his ultimate goal was to be a figure painter. In this he was conforming to the official hierarchy of genres that governed painting at the time.

Pollard birches 1884
pencil, ink and watercolour on paper 39.5 x 54.5 cm

In addition to scenes of weavers and peasants, Van Gogh was attracted to the landscape in and around Nuenen. He wrote to Theo: 'Today I went on a splendid walk for some hours with an acquaintance of mine. [...] I don't say

that nature isn't even more striking and dramatic in Brittany, say, or in Katwijk or the Borinage – yes – but nonetheless the moors and the villages around here are also very, very beautiful, and when I am there I find an inexhaustible treasure-house of subjects from rural life, and the only question is to get to it and work.' Van Gogh regarded this **Pollard birches** 21 as one of his 'mature' drawings. He gave it a title, signed it and sent it and several other pen drawings of the Brabant countryside to his friend Anthon van Rappard, in the hope that he could sell them, 'for he knows quite a few people.'

Peasant woman 1885
oil on canvas 43 x 33.5 cm

'Those women's heads in this part of the world, with the white caps – it is difficult but so eternally beautiful,' Vincent wrote to Theo at the beginning of 1885. 'It is such a delicate tone, particularly the chiaroscuro – the white, and then part of the face in shadow.'

One of the main problems he had had in Drenthe – finding peasants willing to pose for him – seemed almost to resolve itself in Nuenen. It was wintertime, and there was not much work to be done on the land. On top of that, Vincent was the minister's son. The upshot was that he made a large number of studies of the heads of peasants in a short space of time. The De Groot family posed for **The potato eaters** 22. One of the daughters, Gordina, was his favourite model in Nuenen, and at

Pollard birches

Peasant woman

least 20 studies of her are known.
This portrait is one of the few that
Van Gogh signed. He almost certainly
recognised in Gordina the type of
peasant woman that he so admired in
the work of his idol Millet: 'coarse, flat
faces with low foreheads and thick
lips – not that sharp type, but full.'

The potato eaters 1885
oil on canvas 82 x 114 cm

Van Gogh prepared very carefully for
this painting, which was his first
major composition. During the winter
of 1884-85 he made at least 40 drawn
and painted heads of peasant men and
women. In March-April 1885 he began
producing sketches and studies for
'that one of those peasants around a
dish of potatoes.'
Depicting five figures so that their
grouping looks natural is almost
impossible for an unskilled hand, and
Van Gogh made things more difficult
for himself by incorporating different
kinds of lighting effect. The choice of
colour was also daring, for he wanted
to paint a dark interior that had to
appear as bright as possible.
Around 11 April he wrote to Theo:
'Enclosed you will find two scratches
of a few studies I made, and I am also
working again on those peasants
around the dish of potatoes. I have
just come home from that cottage and
have been working at it by lamplight,
though I began it by daylight this
time. This is what the composition
looks like. I painted it on quite a
large canvas, and I think there is
some life in the sketch as it looks

Study for The potato eaters, 1885

The potato eaters

now.' The final painting was completed between the middle of April and the beginning of May and was sent to Theo in Paris.

Van Gogh regarded The potato eaters as a true peasant painting. 'I wanted the canvas to make one think of a way of life quite different from that of we civilised people. Therefore I am not at all anxious for everyone to like it or to admire it immediately.' Van Gogh's first attempt at a masterpiece did not bring him the success he had hoped for, but people did come and view it. Painters, in particular, Theo wrote, 'consider it promising. Some see much beauty in it, precisely because his types are so true. For there is, after all, some truth in it when one says that among the peasant men and women of Brabant there are many more whose faces express the sharp lines of hard toil and poverty than there are who have sweet faces.'

Paris

In the autumn of 1885 Van Gogh left for Antwerp to study at the academy there. He wanted to become a figure painter, which meant that he had to practise drawing from the live model. Disappointed by life at the academy of Antwerp he soon decided to move on to Paris to continue his training in the studio of the painter Fernand Cormon. It was there that Vincent met several fellow artists, among them Henri de Toulouse-Lautrec, Paul Signac and Emile Bernard, who introduced him to the latest developments in art. Through Signac he learned Pointillism, the technique of painting with coloured dots developed by Georges Seurat in 1886. Other artists experimented with a simplified, flat manner of painting with bold outlines around the forms. Vincent adopted these new techniques, but gave them his own, individual stamp. He stayed in Paris until the beginning of 1888.

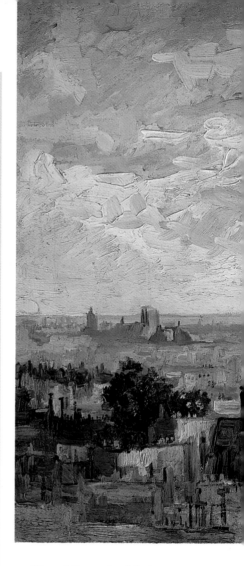

View of the roofs of Paris

View of the roofs of Paris 1886
oil on canvas 54 x 72,5 cm

This panoramic view of Paris was painted after Vincent and Theo had moved to Montmartre, when Van Gogh was spending much of his time out of doors, drawing and painting views of the city.

This one looks south-east over Paris. In the middle, towering over the grey sea of houses, rises the dome of the Panthéon. On the left is Notre-Dame, with the high roof of Saint-Eustache in front of it.
This cityscape is still entirely in the style of the Barbizon painters, so it must have been executed shortly after Van Gogh's arrival in Paris.

View of Paris from Theo's apartment 1887
oil on canvas 46 x 38 cm

'The most remarkable thing about our home is the superb view over the city, with the hills of Meudon, Saint-Cloud and the rest on the horizon, and over it an expanse of sky nearly as great as when one stands on the top of a dune.' Theo wrote this in July 1887 to a

View of Paris

Vase of gladioli

woman friend back in The Hague.
Vincent and he had by then been living for more than a year in the apartment on the Rue Lepic in Montmartre,
then a suburb of Paris. While training
at Cormon's studio Van Gogh had got
to know Paul Signac and his Pointillist
technique, and here he applied that
method of coloured dots in his own
distinctive way. Patiently filling a canvas with tiny dots simply did not suit
his temperament.

Vase of gladioli 1886
oil on canvas 46,5 x 38,5 cm

'I have lacked money for paying
models else I had entirely given
myself to figure painting. But I have
made a series of colour studies in
painting, simply flowers, red poppies,
blue corn flowers and myosotys, white
and rose roses, yellow chrysanthe-
mums – seeking oppositions of blue
with orange, red and green, yellow
and violet, seeking *les tons rompus et*

Boulevard de Clichy

*neutre*s to harmonise brutal extremes.
Trying to render intense colour and
not a grey harmony,' as Van Gogh
wrote to an English friend in 1886.
Colour theories were all the rage
among Paris artists of the day. The
still lifes with flowers and plants that
Van Gogh made in 1886 were mainly
intended as colour studies, as experiments with different colour schemes.
This is confirmed by Theo, who wrote
to his mother in June 1886: 'He is
mainly painting flowers, chiefly in
order to give his next pictures brighter
colours.'
In Paris Van Gogh also got to know
the work of leading 19th-century
flower painters. He admired Henri

Fantin-Latour and, above all, Adolphe
Monticelli, whose broad, thick and suc-
culent strokes of paint he found very
attractive. Something of Monticelli's
influence can be seen in this still life
of gladioli.

Boulevard de Clichy 1887
**pencil, ink and chalk on laid
paper** 40 x 54 cm

Dazzling series of drawings of the
city have survived from Van Gogh's
Paris period. One recurrent theme
was Montmartre, a compact neigh-
bourhood which was growing into
a centre of entertainment. It was
also home to the generation of
artists whom Van Gogh called 'the

'Agostina Segatori

Agostina Segatori in the Café du Tambourin 1887
oil on canvas 55,5 x 46,5 cm

Impressionists of the petit boulevard.'
The Boulevard de Clichy ran just
behind Vincent and Theo's apartment.
Standing on it were the Moulin Rouge,
the famous dance-hall and source of
inspiration for Toulouse-Lautrec, and
the Café du Tambourin, a regular
haunt of the Van Gogh brothers.
Paul Signac and Georges Seurat also
lived on the boulevard.

The woman at this table is believed to
be the Neapolitan Agostina Segatori,
the owner of the café, with whom Van
Gogh may have had a brief affair.
Emile Bernard once said that in
return for meals at the café Vincent
used to pay her with flowers 'that last

Wheatfield with a lark

for ever', still lifes in other words, which were hung on the walls of the café. The setting is certainly the interior of the Café du Tambourin, a bar on the Boulevard de Clichy which numbered Van Gogh and his friends among its regular customers, for the table is shaped like a tambourine.

It was in this café that Van Gogh organised an exhibition of Japanese prints, which he believed had a deep influence on the work of his colleagues Emile Bernard and Louis Anquetin. There is an allusion to this in the background in the shape of a Japanese-looking mural. Other details that appear to echo Japanese prints include the parasol.

Wheatfield with a lark 1887
oil on canvas 54 x 65,5 cm

In the summer of 1887 Van Gogh regularly went out into the countryside around Paris. There, far from the turmoil of the city, he studied and recorded nature: the wind rustling through a wheatfield, for example. These rural subjects were also ideally suited to a colourful palette.

This painting has a remarkably simple structure of three horizontal bands, with the rising lark and a few red poppies among the wheat providing the only accents. The sky, wheat and field of stubble are done with different types of brushstroke.

Paris

Self-portrait

Self-portrait with a straw hat

Self-portrait 1887
oil on cardboard 41 x 33 cm

Self-portrait with a straw hat
1887
oil on cardboard 40,5 x 32,5 cm

Self-portrait with a straw hat
1887
oil on canvas 41 x 31 cm

Self-portrait with a felt hat
1887
oil on canvas 44 x 37,5 cm

Van Gogh painted some 35 self-portraits in the course of his life, no fewer than 27 of them when he was living in Paris. Seventeen of these are now in the Van Gogh Museum.
One of the reasons why Van Gogh immersed himself so deeply in the subject at this time was financial, for he hoped that he could eventually earn money from painting portraits. 'I deliberately bought a good mirror so that if I lacked a model I could work from my own likeness. For if I can succeed in painting the colour of my own face, which is not without difficulty, I shall be able to paint the heads of other men and women.' It also provided him with the opportunity of trying out new techniques and exploring the effects of colour and lighting.
The first series of Paris self-portraits was painted in 1886, when his dark palette still had all the features of the Nuenen period. The next series was made in the summer of 1887, and now some of the paintings have a blue background. Like the flower pieces he was painting at the time, these small portraits are mainly studies of colour and light. One striking feature is the

Self-portrait with a straw hat　　　**Self-portrait with a felt hat**

experimentation with broad, loose brushwork and a thin layer of paint. One of these pictures, the Self-portrait with a felt hat 31, conforms to the popular colour theories of the day and was executed in the modern dotted technique. Van Gogh's innovation was to add strokes around the head in the shape of a halo that gives the picture a particularly forceful effect. This expressive way of painting was 'a real discovery' for Van Gogh.

In addition to experimenting with technique in this series, Van Gogh appears to have been trying to depict his own psyche.

Self-portrait as a painter 1887
oil on canvas 65 x 50,5 cm

'A pinkish-grey face with green eyes, ash-coloured hair, wrinkles on the forehead and around the mouth, stiff, wooden, a very red beard, rather neglected and mournful, but the lips are full, a blue peasant's blouse of coarse linen, and a palette with lemon yellow, vermilion, malachite green, cobalt blue, in short all the colours on the palette except the orange beard, but only whole colours. The figure against a greyish-white wall.' That is how Van Gogh described this Self-portrait as a painter 32 in a letter of January 1888 to his sister Willemien. He had been depressed for some time, and was shortly to leave for Arles. It was the last in the series of Paris self-portraits, and is also the most highly finished one. The full series of 17 small portraits is a superb illustration of Van Gogh's quest for colour, tone, technique and style, which he virtually completed in Paris.

Paris

Self-portrait as a painter

Plaster figure of a horse

Plaster figure illustrating muscles

Plaster figure of a horse
oil on cardboard 33 x 44 cm

Plaster figure illustrating the human muscles
oil on cardboard 35 x 27 cm

Van Gogh had been looking forward to studying with Fernand Cormon, but all told he spent no more than three months in his studio. In addition to many drawings of plaster torsos he made a series of studies in oils of various plaster figurines which are especially interesting for their use of colour. For the background Van Gogh experimented with a bright blue, which was a new shade in his palette.

A few of the original plaster figures have survived, and two of them are illustrated here together with Van Gogh's oil sketches.

Arles

In February 1888 Van Gogh abruptly abandoned the metropolis for the countryside. He moved to the south of France and settled in the small city of Arles, in Provence. His departure may have been prompted by his desire to become a true painter of peasants, but it is also known that he had long been toying with the idea of founding a colony of artists in the south. Another attraction was that he hoped that Provence would provide him with something of the atmosphere that so fascinated him in Japanese prints. The main reason for leaving Paris, though, was that the city had exhausted him – both physically and mentally. As he explained in a letter to his sister Willemien: 'I have observed too often that neither my work nor my health is in very good condition during the winter.' The scenery in the south of France inspired Van Gogh to produce a large number of landscapes, including several of orchards and blossoming fruit trees. The 'maison d'artiste', the artists' colony he had set his heart upon, appeared to be turning into a reality when Gauguin arrived in Arles in October. However, problems arose almost immediately, and after a violent argument on 23 December Gauguin left for Paris. Vincent suffered a nervous breakdown and was hospitalised in Arles.

The pink peach tree

The pink peach tree 1888
oil on canvas 80,5 x 59,5 cm

The white orchard 1888
oil on canvas 60 x 81 cm

The pink orchard 1888
oil on canvas 64,5 x 80,5 cm

In a period of no more than a month, between 24 March and 21 April 1888, Van Gogh painted 14 canvases of blossoming fruit trees in Arles. He hoped that they would sell easily, for 'this kind of subject delights everybody.' While working on the paintings he got the idea of grouping the canvases into decorative ensembles. In April 1888 he wrote to his friend Emile Bernard: 'I am working on nine orchards: one white, one pink, one

The white orchard

The pink orchard

Meadow with flowers near Arles

reddish pink; one white-blue; one greyish pink; one green and pink.' The Van Gogh Museum has three paintings of orchards that were originally intended as an ensemble. The centrepiece of the three, **The pink peach tree** 34, is Van Gogh's second version of the subject. The first is in the Kröller-Müller Museum in Otterlo.

Meadow with flowers near Arles 1888
oil on canvas 54 x 65 cm

On 12 May 1888 Vincent sent Theo a colourful description of a landscape he had just finished. It was 'a meadow full of very yellow buttercups, a ditch full of irises with green leaves and purple flowers, the town in the background, some grey willows, a strip of blue sky. If the meadow does not get mowed I'd like to do this study again, for it was a very beautiful subject and I had some trouble getting the composition right. A little town surrounded by a field all covered with yellow and purple flowers; you know, it is like a Japanese dream.'

Fishing boats on the beach at Les Saintes-Maries-de-la-Mer 1888
oil on canvas 65 x 81,5 cm

Fishing boats on the beach

Arles was not far from the Mediterranean. At the beginning of June Vincent travelled to the fishing village of Les Saintes-Maries-de-la-Mer for a couple of days, and in that short space of time produced no fewer than two seascapes, a view of the village and nine drawings. He wrote to Theo telling him about one of the seascapes: 'I made the drawing of the boats when I went out very early in the morning, and I am now working on a picture based on it, a size 30 canvas with more sea and sky on the right. It was before the boats hastened out; I had watched it every morning, but as they leave very early I didn't have time to paint it.'

To Emile Bernard he described the painting composed in his studio as 'little green, red and blue boats, so pretty in shape and colour that they made one think of flowers.' The Japanese influence in the stylisation of the boats is unmistakable.

The Zouave 1888
oil on canvas 65 x 54 cm

The Zouave 38 is the first in a series of portraits of eye-catching characters that Van Gogh made in Arles. On 21 June he wrote to Theo: 'I have a model at last – a Zouave – a boy with a small face, a bull neck and the eye of a tiger, and I began on one portrait and then began again

The Zouave

on another; the half-length I did of
him was terribly harsh – in a blue uni-
form, the blue of enamel saucepans,
with braids of a faded orange-red, and
two lemon-yellow stars on his breast,
an ordinary blue and very hard to do.
I placed that bronzed, feline head of
his with the reddish cap against a
green door and the orange bricks of
a wall. So it's a savage combination
of incongruous tones, not easy to
manage. The study I made of it seems
very harsh to me, yet I'd always like
to be working on vulgar, even garish
portraits like this. It teaches me something, and that, above all, is what I
want of my work.'
He told Emile Bernard that this portrait was 'hard and utterly ugly and
badly done. All the same, since I tack-
led a real difficulty in it, perhaps it
will pave the way for the future.'

The harvest 1888
oil on canvas 73 x 92 cm

Harvesting wheat provided Van Gogh
with a new subject for a series of

canvases, including several large
ones like The harvest 38.
Within a period of a week, in the sear-
ing heat of mid-June, he made ten
paintings and five drawings of the
subject. The harvest was completed

The harvest

in the studio and given a title, *La mois-
son*. Van Gogh considered it his best
painting yet. 'This canvas absolutely
kills all the others,' he told Theo.

The Yellow House ('The street')
1888
oil on canvas 72 x 91,5 cm

In May 1888 Van Gogh rented four rooms in the right half of the 'Yellow House' on the Place Lamartine in Arles. Before he could move in, though, there was a great deal of refurbishing to be done. Van Gogh was already using the place as a studio, but he wanted to brighten it up with paintings and turn it into a real 'maison

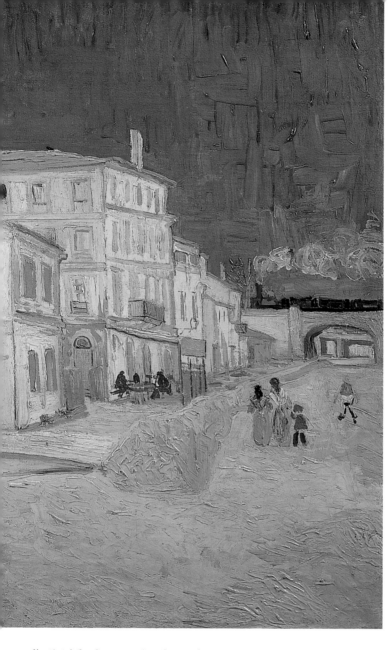

d'artiste'. In the meantime he made this painting, which he called 'The street'. He sent a sketch of it to Theo with the remark: 'It's terrific, these yellow houses in the sun, and the incomparable freshness of the blue. [...] The house on the left is pink with green

The Yellow House

shutters, the one in the shade of the tree. That is the restaurant where I go to eat every day. My friend the postman lives at the end of the street on the left, between the two railway bridges.'

Van Gogh

Arles

The bedroom

The bedroom 1888
oil on canvas 72 x 90 cm

On 16 October 1888 Vincent told his brother about a painting of 'simply my bedroom.' It is a masterpiece, not just for the unusual subject, but also because of the subtle alternation of larger and smaller areas of colour in the three complementary pairs of red and green, yellow and purple, blue and orange. Van Gogh felt that it should be given a white frame, 'as there is no white in the picture.' In September 1889 he made two copies of this painting. One is now in the Arts Institute of Chicago, the other in the Musée d'Orsay in Paris.

Sunflowers 1889
oil on canvas 95 x 73 cm

Van Gogh had planned a series of decorative paintings for the interior of his 'Yellow House' so that he could receive his colleague Paul Gauguin in style. The house was to be a 'studio of refuge' and a 'maison d'artiste'. Knowing that Gauguin liked his paintings of sunflowers he decided to design a series of still lifes of them which should be framed in 'thin strips of wood painted with orange lead'. He immersed himself in the subject 'with the enthusiasm of a Marseillais eating bouillabaisse', but eventually completed two still lifes, one with a yellow background, the other blue-turquoise. The former is now in the National Gallery in London.

He later wrote to Theo: 'As you will see, these canvases catch the eye. [...] It is a kind of painting that rather changes to the eye, and becomes richer the longer one looks at it.' In January 1889 Van Gogh made three copies of these two still lifes, which he described as 'absolutely identical replicas.' The copy with the yellow background is the one in the Van Gogh Museum.

Rock with trees: Montmajour
1888
pencil and Indian ink 49 x 61 cm

About five kilometres north-east of Arles stand the majestic ruins of the medieval abbey of Montmajour. Van Gogh discovered them soon after he arrived in Arles.
At the beginning of March he wrote to Theo about 'a ruined abbey on a hill covered with holly, pines and grey olives. We'll have a go at that soon, I hope.'

Rock with trees: Montmajour

Sunflowers

Saint-Rémy

At the end of April 1889 Van Gogh decided to become a voluntary patient at the mental asylum of Saint-Paul-de-Mausole in the village of Saint-Rémy, near Arles. There he was treated by Dr Peyron, who allowed him to continue working and even provided him with a studio. The asylum garden inspired Van Gogh to paint irises and lilacs. He also made paintings and drawings of the walled wheatfield he could see from his window. Sometimes he worked under supervision outside the institution, which is where the paintings of olive trees and cypresses were executed.

Van Gogh's illness, which made him prone to fits, often prevented him from working for long periods. It was around now that his work began to be spoken of in slightly wider circles. The critic Albert Aurier wrote an enthusiastic article about him in the 'Mercure de France'.

The reaper 1889
oil on canvas 73 x 92 cm

Van Gogh made three versions of this painting. The first, a nature study, dates from June 1889 and is now in the Kröller-Müller Museum in Otterlo. 'The canvas is all yellow,' Van Gogh wrote, 'except for the wall and the background of purple hills.' The painting was meant to express 'the intense heat' – an effect that was achieved by using a lot of bright yellow.

In September, in his studio, Van Gogh began on a second version of 'the little reaper under the big sun,' which is the one in the Van Gogh Museum. A third Reaper, which he painted for his mother at the end of September, is a small copy of the one in Amsterdam. Van Gogh explained his choice of the simple subject of the reaper using biblical imagery: 'For I see in this reaper – a vague figure fighting like a devil in the midst of the heat to get to the end of his task – I see in him the image of death, in the sense that humanity stands for the wheat he is reaping.'

The garden of the Saint Paul's hospital 1889
oil on canvas 71,5 x 90,5 cm

'Beneath the trees, empty stone benches, dark box trees; the sky is mirrored – yellow – in a puddle left by the rain. A sunbeam, the last ray of daylight, raises the sombre ochre almost to orange.' This was how Van Gogh described his Garden of the Saint Paul's hospital 74 to Emile Bernard. He went on: 'You will understand that the combination of red-ochre, of green gloomed over by grey, the black streaks defining the contours, produces the sensation of anguish called "noir-rouge" from which some of my companions in misfortune suffer from time to time. Moreover, the motif of the great tree struck by lightning, the sickly green-

The reaper

The garden of the Saint Paul's hospital

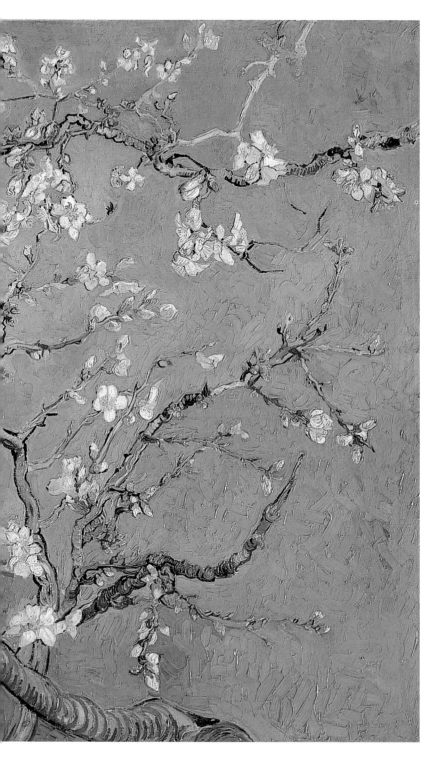

Van Gogh

Saint-Rémy

Almond blossom

Reaper

Sheaf-binder

pink smile of the last flower of autumn serve to confirm this impression.'

Almond blossom 1890
oil on canvas 73,5 x 92 cm

Van Gogh painted these branches in honour of his infant nephew and namesake, the son of Theo and Jo, who was born in the spring of 1890. It was intended for the parents' bedroom. Vincent wrote: 'A day or two ago I started painting a picture for him of a great blue sky with branches full of blossoms standing out against it. It is not impossible that I shall see him soon – at least I hope so – towards the end of the month.'

Vase of irises 1890
oil on canvas 92 x 73,5 cm

In the spring of 1890 Van Gogh completed an incredible number of canvases. The irises belong to a series

of four flower paintings which were undoubtedly meant to be a decorative ensemble, just like the sunflowers he had done in Arles. Van Gogh said that the use of colour was 'an effect of tremendously disparate complementaries, which strengthen each other by their juxtaposition.'

Reaper (after Millet) 1889
oil on canvas 44 x 33 cm

Sheaf-binder (after Millet)
1889
oil on canvas 44,5 x 32 cm

In September 1889 Van Gogh made ten small paintings after prints of rural activities by Millet. He copied the black-and-white prints faithfully and then coloured them – blue and yellow, the tints he associated with life on the land. Seven of those ten pictures are now in the Van Gogh Museum.

Vase of irises

Auvers-sur-Oise

On 20 May 1890, Van Gogh travelled from Paris to Auvers-sur-Oise, a small village some 30 kilometres to the northwest. It was here that he spent the last seventy days of his life. He became very friendly with the local doctor, Paul Gachet, who was also an amateur painter. Gachet had been a friend of Monticelli, and had built up a collection of paintings that included works by Cézanne, Renoir and Pissarro, whom he knew personally.

Rural Auvers was an artists' village, and among the painters who had lived there were Cézanne, Pissarro, Daubigny and Daumier – all of whom Van Gogh greatly admired. Vincent was delighted with Auvers. Gachet taught him how to etch, which resulted in a portrait of the doctor. He also made close-up studies of stalks of wheat, which he described to Gauguin as: 'nothing but ears of wheat with green-blue stalks, long leaves like ribbons, green shot through with pink.'

His enthusiasm for the north of France was short-lived, however. On 27 July he shot himself in the chest. He died of his wounds two days later, with his brother Theo by his bedside.

View of Auvers 1890
oil on canvas 50 x 52 cm

Old vineyard with a peasant woman 1890
pencil and watercolour 43,5 x 45 cm

Quite soon after he had arrived in Auvers Vincent wrote to Theo: 'I am very well at the moment and am working hard, have four painted studies and two drawings. You will see a drawing of an old vineyard with the figure of a peasant woman. I intend to make a big canvas of it.' However, he never got around to a painted version of this Old vineyard with a peasant woman 53. There are numerous drawn and painted landscapes with houses and cottages from the beginning of Van Gogh's time in Auvers. A distinctive feature of northern French villages at that time were the houses with moss-grown thatched roofs. He remarked on them in a letter to Theo of 20 May. 'Auvers is very beautiful, among other things a lot of old thatched roofs, which are getting rare. So I should hope that by settling down to do some canvases of this there would be a chance of recovering the expenses of my stay – for really it is profoundly beautiful, it is the real countryside, classic and picturesque.' He wrote to his sister Willemien around the same time: 'As for myself, at the moment I am still fearful of the noise and bustle of Paris, and I immediately left for the country – to an old village. Here there are moss-covered thatched roofs which are superb, and I am certainly going to do something with them.'

View of Auvers

Old vineyard with a peasant woman

**Wheatfield under
thunderclouds** 1890
oil on canvas 50 x 100,5 cm

Wheatfield with crows 1890
oil on canvas 50,5 x 103 cm

Van Gogh depicted vast fields with
birds in the sky at every season of the
year. As early as his Paris period he
had painted an idyllic impression of a
Wheatfield with a lark 29. People
sometimes see these late wheatfields
as harbingers of Van Gogh's approach-

Wheatfield under thunderclouds

ing end. It is true that his last letters
were sombre. He wrote to his brother
about 'vast fields of wheat under trou-
bled skies,' and said that he did not
need to go out of his way 'to express
sadness and extreme loneliness' in
them. But despite his despondent
mood, he also had this to say about
these landscapes: 'I am almost certain
that I have expressed in these canvases what I cannot put into words, name-
ly how healthy and invigorating I find
the countryside.'

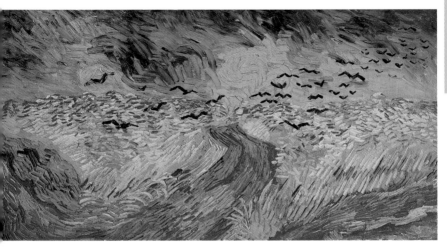

Wheatfield with crows

Cover of *Paris Illustré*,
'Le Japon', May 1886

Tracing made from 'Paris Illustré'

Van Gogh's Japan

Japanese prints

'I envy the Japanese that great clarity that all things have for them. Their work is as simple as breathing, and they make a figure with a few sure strokes, as if it were as simple as buttoning one's waistcoat.'

Vincent van Gogh 1888

One very special section of the museum's holdings is the collection of some 500 Japanese prints that Vincent and Theo put together in Paris. Vincent had first come across this form of oriental art in Antwerp. In November 1885 he wrote to Theo: 'My studio is not bad, especially as I have pinned a lot of little Japanese prints on the wall, which amuse me very much. You know, those little women's figures in gardens or on the beach, horsemen, flowers, knotty thorn branches.'

In Paris those prints took on a different function for Van Gogh, providing him with an important source of inspiration for his own experiments in stylising a composition. In the spring of 1887 he organised an exhibition of his Japanese prints in the Café du Tambourin. That same year he made three copies after Japanese models: **The courtesan** 57, **Bridge in the rain** 58 and **The flowering plum tree** 59. After he went to live in Arles Van Gogh announced that he no longer needed the Japanese prints, because all he had to do was keep his eyes open. As he explained at the beginning of June 1888: 'Your perception changes after a while, you look more as the Japanese do, you experience colour differently.'

The courtesan (after Kesai Eisen) 1887
oil on canvas 105.5 x 60.5 cm

Tracing made from 'Paris Illustré' 1887
pencil and ink on transparent paper 39 x 25 cm

The courtesan, unlike Van Gogh's two other 'Japonaiseries,' as they were called, was not copied from a woodcut

The courtesan

but from an illustration on the cover of *Paris Illustré* of May 1886, a double issue devoted to Japan. For the border around the courtesan Van Gogh designed a broad strip with a pond filled with waterlilies and bamboo stalks. The cranes and frogs may be references to the woman's profession, for 'grue' and 'grenouilles' were common synonyms for prostitutes. Van Gogh took the cranes from a print by Sato Torakiyo.

Bridge in the rain (after Hiroshige) 1887
oil on canvas 73 x 54 cm

In the summer or autumn of 1887 Van Gogh made two copies after famous woodcuts by Utagawa Hiroshige (1797–1858) that he had in his collection. One important difference with the original prints is the powerful use of colour and contrasts. Van Gogh also gave his canvases bright borders decorated with calligraphic characters borrowed from other Japanese prints.

The flowering plum tree (after Hiroshige) 1887
oil on canvas 55 x 46 cm

Utagawa Hiroshige 1797–1858
The flowering plum tree in the garden of the teahouse at Kameido 1857
woodcut 34 x 22.5 cm

Tracing of Hiroshige's woodcut 'The flowering plum tree'
pencil and ink on transparent paper 38 x 25.8 cm

Hiroshige's woodcut of a flowering plum tree in the garden of the teahouse at Kameido would have particularly appealed to Van Gogh for its dramatic contrast between foreground and background.
He carefully copied the huge close-up of a branch in the foreground for his own Flowering plum tree 59. This can be seen from the tracing on squared paper, which made it very easy for Van Gogh to transfer the scene onto canvas.

The flowering plum tree

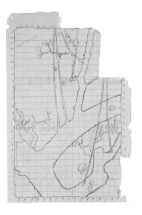

Hiroshige (left); Tracing of Hiroshige's woodcut (right)

Documents

Letters and sketchbooks

'I wrote to you already, early this morning, then I went out to work on a picture of a park in the sunshine. I then brought it back home and went out again with a blank canvas, and that too is finished. And now I want to write to you again.'

Vincent van Gogh September 1888

In addition to almost 750 of Van Gogh's letters the museum has a collection of documents by and about Vincent van Gogh. They include his scrapbooks, some poetry albums and a collection of hundreds of magazine illustrations that he used as aids in learning his craft. The museum also has numerous groups of letters relating to Theo van Gogh and other members of the family.

The most important documents, of course, are the letters that Vincent wrote to his brother Theo, to his mother, and his sister Willemien. The letters to Theo were first published in three volumes in 1914, on the instigation of Jo van Gogh-Bonger. Her son oversaw a new edition in 1953, which also included the letters to Anthon van Rappard and Emile Bernard. In 1990 a four-volume edition was published to mark the centenary of Van Gogh's death. It is the first Dutch translation of all the letters by and to the artist.

A scholarly edition of the letters will be completed around the year 2000. This is a joint project involving the Van Gogh Museum and the Constantijn Huygens Institute in The Hague. The texts of the letters will be published in their original, unabridged form, accompanied by an explanatory commentary.

Vincent first wrote to Theo in August 1872, when he was 19 and his brother 15. The last letter was written in July 1890. In the intervening eighteen years Vincent wrote at least ninehundred letters, probably even more. That comes to around three a month, but the frequency was rather variable. More important than the actual number of letters is their average length. As the correspondence grew, so did the size of each letter – often running to eight pages or more. It is thanks to these documents that one can get to know Van Gogh in every aspect of his developing personality. It is a marvellously rich vein of material that seems to do away with the need for a biography. He wrote the way other people keep a diary, with news about everyday events, comments on books, art and artists, revelations about his expectations of life, and his fears about illness and death. All of this was written in his highly personal, expressive style. The following quotations show just what a great epistolary talent he was.

Letter to Theo, c. 3 October 1883

Letter to Theo, 28 October 1883

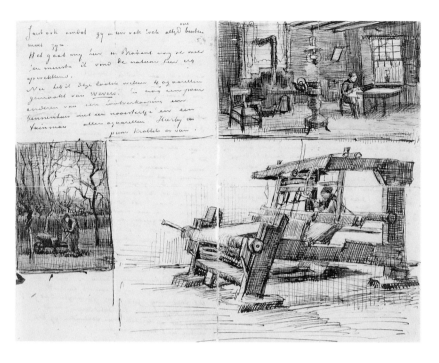

Letter to Theo, January 1884

In a letter written to Theo from The Hague on Sunday evening, 22 July 1883, Vincent confesses his doubts about the course he had embarked upon. He also tries to explain what his close relationship with Theo means to him.

'In fact, I have no real friend but you, and when I am in low spirits I always think of you. I only wish you were here, that we might again talk together about moving to the country. [...] I have again had to pay out money right and left – landlord, paint, baker, grocer, shoemaker, heaven knows what – and only a little is left. Ah well, but the worst of it is that after many such weeks one sometimes feels one's strength ebbing and succumbs to a pervading feeling of weariness. [...] I worked a little today, but was suddenly overcome by a deep depression which I cannot exactly account for. It is at such moments that one wishes one were made of iron, and detests being merely flesh and blood. I had written to you early this morning, but after I had mailed the letter it suddenly seemed as if all my troubles came crowding in together, and it became too much for me because I could no longer look clearly into the future. I can't put it any other way, and I can't understand why I shouldn't succeed in my work. I have put all my heart into it, and, for a moment at least, that seemed to me a mistake. But, old chap, you know it yourself – to what, in practice, in real life, must one devote one's strength and life and mental effort to? One must take a risk and say, I will do a certain thing and see it through. It may turn out

wrong now and again, and one may run into a blank wall if people do not care for it; but after all one needn't care, need one? I don't think one should worry about it, but sometimes it all becomes too much, and one feels miserable, even if one wishes otherwise.'

Letter to Theo, 13 October 1888

Van Gogh's letters also shed a light on his views about the art and artists of his day. In one to Emile Bernard, written in Paris in the autumn of 1887, he criticised the latter's rejection of Paul Signac and his experiments with Pointillism.

'If you have quarrelled with a painter, and consequently say: "I shall withdraw my picture if Signac exhibits where I exhibit," and if you act patronisingly towards him, then it seems to me that you are not behaving as well as you might. For it is better to look at something for a long time before delivering such a categorical judgment, and to think things over. For when there is a disagreement reflection shows us as many wrongs on our part as on the other's – and that the latter has as much *raison d'être* as we would wish for ourselves. So if you have already thought that Signac and others who use Pointillism do, in fact, quite often make very fine things, then instead of being disparaging you must respect those things and speak of them sympathetically, especially if there has been a quarrel. Otherwise you yourself become sectarian and narrow-minded, and the equal of those who utterly despise others and believe themselves to be the only ones who are in the right.'

An important part of the letters consists of passages in which Van Gogh describes the drawings and paintings he was working on at the time, and what it was that made him choose a specific subject. In addition to comments on composition and the use of colour, he often enclosed sketches to give his correspondents 'an idea of it.'

At first those sketches were inserted loose in the letters. A letter sent from Drenthe in early October 1883 was accompanied by a sheet of sketches with observations of peasant women in local costume and views of the Drenthe countryside, 'accentuated here and there by a shed of turf sods or a small farm, or a few scrawny birches' 60. One little drawing of a peasant harrowing a field 62 was intended to illustrate his view of the task of being an artist. 'One must undertake it with confidence that one is doing something reasonable, just as the farmer guides his plough, or like our friend in the scratch below, who is harrowing, and even drags the harrow himself. If one hasn't a horse, one is one's own horse – as many people are here.'

In letters from Nuenen written at the beginning of January 1884 Van Gogh repeatedly added sketches of weavers 63, the subject that was preoccupying him then. 'Things are going quite well with me here in Brabant, at least I find the nature here very stimulating. The past few weeks I have made four watercolours of weavers. I enclose a couple of scratches of them.'

He also kept Theo informed about his latest works when he was living in the south of France. One letter that he sent his brother from Arles in the autumn of 1888 contained several fine sketches 64. He described the colours in order to give Theo a better idea of what he had done. 'The Trinquetaille bridge with all these steps is a canvas done on a grey morning, the stones, the asphalt, the pavements are grey; the sky pale blue; the figures, coloured; and there is a sickly tree with yellow foliage.'

Henri de Toulouse-Lautrec, Portrait of Vincent van Gogh, 1887

19th century

Paintings and drawings

'He has not yet sold any paintings, but exchanges them for others. In this way we are building up a fine collection, which is worth something in itself, of course.'

Theo van Gogh June 1886

A not unimportant part of the collection in the Van Gogh Museum consists of works by Vincent's contemporaries. The nucleus is formed by the paintings, drawings and prints collected by Theo and Vincent themselves. It was mainly when Vincent was living with Theo in Paris that their plan to form a true artist's collection took shape. Thanks to Theo's contacts on the art market and Vincent's acquaintance with artists, the brothers' initially modest collection grew rapidly. It never became a fully rounded whole, however, for they were not granted the time.

Van Gogh had met Louis Anquetin, Emile Bernard and Henri de Toulouse-Lautrec at Fernand Cormon's studio. Theo occasionally bought work from artists whom he represented, such as Camille Pissarro, Armand Guillaumin and, later, Paul Gauguin. There are works by all them in the collection, and they were acquired by exchange or purchase.

The brothers also had paintings by earlier but much-loved artists like Adolphe Monticelli and Henri Fantin-Latour.

Major gaps in the collection have been filled in the past decade. Louis Anquetin, Georges Seurat and Paul Signac, friends of Van Gogh, are now represented in the museum, as are older painters whom Van Gogh admired, such as the 'peasant painters' Jules Breton and Léon hermitte. The museum also has several works by Puvis de Chavannes, a painter with a classical bent in whom Van Gogh became interested towards the end of his life.

A start has also been made on forming a group of Symbolist artists from around the turn of the century, which now includes Odilon Redon, Fernand Khnopff, Maurice Denis and Edmond Aman-Jean. Dutch artists from the end of the 19th century who can be associated with Van Gogh, like Matthijs Maris, George Breitner and Jan Sluijters, have also been added to the collection.

In this way the Van Gogh Museum has rapidly grown into an institution embodying the great variety in styles that was a hallmark of the second half of the 19th century. Van Gogh, though, remains the focal point.

Circle of friends Realism Symbolism Dutchmen Sculpture

Circle of friends

**Living in the same neighbour-
hood as Vincent and Theo van
Gogh in Paris were a number
of Impressionist and Post-
Impressionist artists.
Edgar Degas and Claude Monet,
the first of the Impressionists,
were already recognised mas-
ters whose work was in some
demand by 1886, when Van
Gogh arrived in Paris. Emile
Bernard, Paul Signac and Paul
Gauguin – men of Van Gogh's
generation – were engaged on
a search for new painting techniques, for different subjects
and for fresh sources of inspiration in exotic countries.**

Emile Bernard 1868–1941
**Self-portrait with a portrait
of Gauguin** 1888
oil on canvas 46.5 x 55.5 cm

Charles Laval 1862–1894
Self-portrait 1888
oil on canvas 50 x 60 cm

The most close-knit group of paintings in Vincent and Theo's art collection consists of the self-portraits that
Gauguin, Bernard and Laval sent to
Van Gogh in Arles in exchange for
works painted by him.
Vincent had gone to Arles to escape
the clamour of Paris and in order to
found an artists' colony in the south
of France where he and his friends
could work together. The exchange
of paintings was part of that Utopian
ideal. Vincent eagerly looked forward
to the arrival of Emile Bernard and
Paul Gauguin, but when there were
delays he asked them to send portraits
of each other. Instead they both produced self-portraits that contained a
small portrait of the other one in the
background. The portraits are dedicated
to 'son copaing Vincent' (Bernard) and
'l'ami Vincent' (Gauguin). Charles
Laval, whose self-portrait also arrived
in Arles, was not known to Vincent
but was a close friend of Gauguin
and was staying in Pont-Aven at the
time. Van Gogh was particularly
impressed by Bernard's canvas, which
he described as 'a few simple tones, a
few dark lines, but it has the elegance
of a real, true Manet.'
Around 16 November Vincent wrote to
his brother: 'You will also be pleased
to hear that we have an addition to
the collection of artists' portraits. [...]
The portrait of Laval is very bold, very
distinguished, and will be precisely
one of the pictures you speak of, those
one gets hold of before other people
have recognised the talent.'

Paul Gauguin 1848–1903
**Self-portrait with a portrait
of Bernard, 'Les misérables'**
1888
oil on canvas 45 x 55 cm

In this self-portrait Gauguin refers
to *Les misérables*, the famous novel
by Victor Hugo which Van Gogh had
also read. Gauguin identified with
the principal character, the escaped
criminal Jean Valjean, because he
too felt rejected by society.

Bernard, Self-portrait with a portrait of Gauguin

Laval, Self-portrait

les misérables

àttous Vincent

P Gauguin 88

Gauguin, Self-portrait with a portrait of Bernard, 'Les misérables'

Paul Gauguin 1848–1903
Picking fruit on Martinique,
'Négresses' 1887
oil on canvas 89 x 116 cm

Gauguin already had something of
a reputation as an artistic innovator
when Van Gogh met him in November 1887, shortly after his return from
Martinique.
Gauguin, the son of a French journal-
ist and a Creole mother, had gone to
Panama in April that year, together
with Charles Laval. After a short stay
they travelled on to the island of
Martinique. Gauguin was captivated by
the idyllic life of the local population
but soon discovered the less attractive
sides of 'primitive' life. He caught
dysentery and hastened back to Paris.

Theo and Vincent bought 'Négresses'
for their own collection. Van Gogh
described it to his sister Willemien
in a letter of July 1888: 'Some time
ago Theo bought a large picture
from him of negresses in pink, blue,
orange and yellow cotton dresses
under tamarind, coconut and banana
trees, with the sea in the distance.'

Georges Seurat 1859–1891
The Seine near Courbevoie
1883-84
oil on panel 15,5 x 24,5 cm

Van Gogh's Paris period (1886-1887)
coincided with Georges Seurat's ascen-
dancy as the leading figure of the

avant-garde. Seurat worked in a completely new technique that later became known as Pointillism. However, he also painted in a more Impressionist style, as in this small panel of the river Seine near the Paris suburb of Courbevoie, which is done with short strokes of bright colour. Seurat made numerous small studies of this kind, which fitted neatly into the paint-box that he carried with him when working out of doors. The studies were generally used to prepare for his large, more refined and detailed Pointillist canvases, but some are works of art in their own right.

Georges Seurat 1859–1891
Singer in a café-chantant,
'The Eden concert' 1887
black conté crayon and pastel
29,5 x 22,5 cm

Seurat, The Seine near Courbevoie

'I congratulate you on purchasing the Seurat; you must make another attempt to arrange an exchange with Seurat with what I shall send you.' This was Vincent's reaction in early March 1888 to Theo's news that he had got this drawing for a bargain price. Van Gogh had met Seurat in Paris shortly before and had a high opinion of him, although he did not find his Pointillist technique entirely convincing.

Seurat's Singer in a café-chantant 74 was first exhibited at the Salon des Indépendants in 1887. Cafés-chantants were immensely popular at the time, not only with people looking for entertainment but with painters as well.

Seurat, Singer

Claude Monet 1840–1927
**Bulb-fields and windmills
near Rijnsburg** 1886
oil on canvas 65 x 81 cm

In 1886, on a nine-day visit to Holland at the invitation of an admirer, Monet made a series of five paintings of bulb-fields. He found the flowers 'amazingly beautiful,' but felt that they would drive a poor painter mad: 'It can't be done with our palette,' he said. Van Gogh very probably saw the bulb-fields at an exhibition in a Paris gallery in the early summer of 1886.
A year later this painting was placed on commission with the Boussod & Valadon gallery, that is to say with Theo van Gogh. It was sold to a foreign buyer, and after a detour eventually arrived in Holland. It now

Monet, Bulb-fields and windmills

hangs in the museum on loan from the Netherlands Institute for cultural heritage in Amsterdam.

Paul Signac 1863–1935
Railway junction near
Bois-Colombes
'Gare d'Asnières' 1885
oil on canvas 46.4 x 65 cm

Paul Signac was the first well-known
artist to become a friend of Vincent

van Gogh's in Paris. They often went
out painting together in Asnières, a
suburb of Paris. Signac knew Georges
Seurat and had fallen under the spell
of Pointillism. Although Van Gogh
learned this manner of painting, and
appreciated it, he was more excited
by Signac's earlier, Impressionist
work.

Signac, Railway junction near Bois-Colombes

This painting shows precisely what Signac was after. He championed the art of the 'unpicturesque.' At first sight not a single object in this picture seems especially worth painting. Van Gogh borrowed the motif of the truncated poles and the undulating fencing in his own work.

The museum did not have a work by Signac until it bought this Railway junction near Bois-Colombes 76 in 1986.

Camille Pissarro 1830–1903
Landscape with a rainbow
1889
gouache on paper 30 x 60 cm

On 12 December 1889 Camille Pissarro wrote to Theo van Gogh: 'A landscape with a rainbow is for Madame van Gogh, and I would ask you to be so kind as to present it to her on my behalf and convey my very best wishes for the new year.'

The fan-shaped gouache was Pissarro's way of thanking Theo for the help he had given him at a time when he was short of money. Pissarro, initially an Impressionist who sold well, had begun working in the Pointillist style. This led to a clash with his art dealer, Durand-Ruel, who found it difficult to sell this new work. Theo van Gogh was not so commercially minded and supported Pissarro, although with little success.

Henri de Toulouse-Lautrec
1864–1901
Young woman at a table, 'Poudre de riz' 1887
oil on canvas 56 x 46 cm

Van Gogh met Henri de Toulouse-Lautrec, who was more than ten years his junior, at Cormon's studio in 1886. The following year Lautrec made a profile portrait 66 of Van Gogh sitting in a café.

Many of Lautrec's subjects were taken from the seamier side of modern life: cafés, brothels, music halls and cabarets. Women seated at café tables were also depicted by painters like Manet and Renoir.

It is not clear where this particular woman is sitting. On the table in front of her is a small red pot of rice-powder, *poudre de riz*, which was used to give the face a pale, elegant complexion. This is probably a portrait of Suzanne Valadon, Lautrec's former lover.

The painting was first shown in February 1888 at the annual exhibition of Les Vingt, a group of artists in Brussels. The catalogue lists it as 'poudre de riz. A M. Van Gogh.'

It belonged to Theo van Gogh, who had bought it on 12 January 1888 for 150 guilders for the collection of paintings that he and his brother were so enthusiastically putting together.

Pissarro, Landscape with a rainbow

Toulouse-Lautrec, Young woman at a table

Realism

Van Gogh's great idols were Jean-François Millet, Jules Breton and Léon Lhermitte – French painters of peasant life. He particularly admired Millet, whose peasant genre he considered to be 'the very heart of modern art'. He set out to emulate his great predecessor with The potato eaters 22 in Nuenen, and later with his own Sower 47 in Arles, taking Millet as his yardstick for painting in which 'all reality is simultaneously a symbol'. He also respected Jules Breton as a poet; calling him 'the voice of the wheat.'

The Van Gogh Museum still does not have a Millet in its collection, but in 1988 it acquired Breton's Young peasant girl with a hoe 85, and in 1991 Lhermitte's Haymaking 82.

Realism is not restricted to scenes of peasants. The museum has two paintings by Jean-François Raffaëlli, the painter of 'urban workers'. Felician von Myrbach is represented with The print shop 87, Thomas Couture with A Realist 84, which pokes fun at Realism, and Philippe Rousseau with two still-life paintings.

Henri Harpignies 1819–1916
View of the Château d'Hérisson 1871
oil on canvas 41.2 x 63.5 cm

Harpignies was a landscape painter from the school of Jean Baptiste Corot (1796–1875). Whereas Corot set out to create atmospheric effects in his landscapes, Harpignies worked with harsh contrasts between light and shade. The critic Théophile Gautier said of him: 'Monsieur Harpignies draws a neat contour around each object, his trees, rocks and meadows, and fills them with daring, stiff and arbitrary brushstrokes.' The museum bought this painting in 1995.

Harpignies, Château d'Hérisson

Léon Augustin Lhermitte
1844–1925
Haymaking 1887
oil on canvas 216 x 264 cm

Léon Lhermitte was a shining example to Van Gogh, who recognised in him someone who 'knows the sturdy, stern workman's figure thoroughly, and takes his subjects from the very heart of the people.' Van Gogh used reproductions of his paintings to help

him when he was painting **The potato eaters** 22. He told Theo that Lhermitte was the master of the figure in everything he did, and even compared him to Rembrandt. In his eyes the Frenchman 'perfectly satisfies all that honesty demands.' In 1887 Lhermitte signed a fixed contract with the Boussod, Valadon & Cie gallery, where Theo worked, but Theo and Vincent had no painting by him in their collection.

Lhermitte, Haymaking

Couture, A Realist

Thomas Couture 1815–1879
A Realist 1865
oil on canvas 46 x 38 cm

Thomas Couture supplied his own explanation of this satirical painting: 'I am depicting the interior of a modern studio; it has nothing in common with those of earlier periods, in which you always find fragments of the finest classical sculptures. [...] But thanks to artistic progress nowadays I have little to depict, because we have the simplest attributes and, moreover, we have changed gods. The Laocoon has been replaced by a cabbage, the feet of the Gladiator by a candlestick dripping tallow, or by a shoe.'
Here he has summed up his criticism of the Realists. He felt that they had no feeling for lofty themes and were incapable of depicting their subjects in a refined way.

Breton, Young peasant girl

Jules Breton 1827–1905
**Young peasant girl with a
hoe** 1882
oil on canvas 51.5 x 46 cm

This pensive peasant girl is such a
monumental presence in the foreground that she appears to transcend
the everyday life of the countryside.
Remarking on Breton's attractive
models, who are often depicted in
classical poses, Millet once said that
Breton always painted village girls

who wouldn't be staying around very
long.
One thing that Millet and Breton had
in common was that they both lived
in the country for much of their
lives, which enabled them to observe
peasant life from close at hand. With
its combination of idealised scenes
set against realistic backgrounds,
Breton's work was regarded as the
refined counterpart of the far more
rustic-looking Millet.

Jean-François Raffaëlli 1850–1924
The veterans c. 1884
oil on panel 56.8 x 39.9 cm

It was said of Raffaëlli that he was the poet of the humble. He was compared to Millet in the sense that what the latter did for the land in his paintings Raffaëlli did for the modest people of Paris.

The young Seurat, Signac and Bernard regarded him as the discoverer of the Paris suburbs, the new districts that held such an attraction for them. Van Gogh, too, who knew Raffaëlli's work

mainly from illustrated magazines, valued him as the urban variant of Millet, 'straight from the heart of the urban workers.'

Theo van Gogh exhibited work by Raffaëlli in the summer of 1890, and there are several prints by him in Theo and Vincent's collection which may have been acquired on that occasion. The purchase of The veterans 86 in 1990 and a self-portrait in 1992 added a painting and a pastel to that interesting group.

Felician Freiherr von Myrbach-Rheinfeld 1853–1940
A print shop 1884
oil on canvas 64.5 x 80.9 cm

One of the countless foreign artists drawn to Paris in the 19th century was the Austrian nobleman Felician von Myrbach. He made his debut at the Salon in 1883, and the following year he exhibited this Print shop there under the title *Chez l'imprimeur en taille-douce*. Particularly appealing features are the beautiful way in which the light falls into the room and the rhythmical composition of the levers of the printing presses. Von Myrbach-Rheinfeld was best-known in Paris as an illustrator. He worked for *Paris Illustré*, which was published by the Boussod, Valadon & Cie gallery. The museum acquired this painting in 1992.

Realism

87

Symbolism

Symbolism made its appearance in the visual arts chiefly in the 1890s. One of the characteristics of Symbolist artists is that they preferred to visualise their thoughts and ideas rather than depict visible reality.
The museum has recently been devoting considerable attention to this movement after acquiring several pastels by Odilon Redon. Since then works by Maurice Denis, Fernand Khnopff, François Aman-Jean, Carlos Schwabe and others have been assembled around that core group.

Denis, The two sisters

Maurice Denis 1870–1941
The two sisters 1891
oil on canvas 40.5 x 32.5 cm

'Remember that a painting, before being a war-horse or a nude woman or genre scene, is essentially a flat surface covered with colours assembled in a certain order.' This much-quoted observation is from a manifesto of 1890 by Maurice Denis in which he argued that form and colour should be the means of expression, rather than the realistic or narrative content of paintings that was so popular at the time. In 1888, Denis was one of the founders of the Symbolist group known as the Nabis.
This close-up of two women is the central section of what was once a much larger work inspired by Maurice Maeterlinck's stage play, *L'intruse*. The simplified shapes and unnatural

colours, which appear to be derived from Japanese prints, give the work a haunting delicacy.
The museum acquired The two sisters 88 in 1991 to strengthen the group of Symbolist painters in the collection.

Odilon Redon 1840–1916
'La barque' c. 1897
pastel 44.2 x 28 cm

The Van Gogh Museum has two pastels that once belonged to Andries Bonger, Theo van Gogh's brother-in-law. Bonger acquired 'La barque' 89 in 1902 from the collection of the sculptress Saar de Swart, who had been given it by the artist in December 1898.

Redon, 'La barque'

Maris, The girl with the goats

Redon was deliberately vague about
the meaning of his works. He
described this enigmatic pastel as:
'Sombre, brown light with purple and
red clouds; on the left a being with a
halo on a barque, tufts of gold by the
bow of the barque, and on the waters
a kind of fluorescent blue like a will-
o'-the-wisp.'

Matthijs Maris 1839–1917
The girl with the goats 1875
oil on canvas 65 x 101.5 cm

Khnopff, Portrait of Achille Lerminiaux

With his dreamy paintings, Matthijs
Maris was an eccentric among his contemporaries, the painters of the Hague
School. Van Gogh met him in Paris in
1875, when he was socially and artisti-
cally isolated. Years later, in May 1885,
he recalled that meeting: 'If they hadn't
made Thijs Maris too wretched and
melancholy to work he might have
found something wonderful. I think of
that fellow so often, Theo, because his
work is so marvellous. It is dreaminess
– but what a master!'

François Aman-Jean 1860–1935
**Portrait of Thadée Caroline
Jacquet** c. 1892
oil on canvas 55.2 x 46.1 cm

The painter Aman-Jean is best
known for his portraits of women in
frozen poses. In this canvas he painted his fiancée in 'lost profile,' which
heightens the languid mood of the
picture.

Fernand Khnopff 1858–1921
**Portrait of the violinist
Achille Lerminiaux** 1885
pastel 16.6 x 16.6 cm

Aman-Jean, Portrait

The Belgian Symbolist Fernand
Khnopff is known chiefly for his
depictions of *femmes fatales*, with the
features of mysterious sphinxes or
Medusa's.
He also made portraits of his artist
friends, many of them in the pastel
technique, which lent itself to an
evocative sense of concealment.
The small pastel portrait of 1885
shows the violinist Achille Lerminiaux
with his eyes closed, engaged in a
dialogue with his muse from which
the viewer is excluded.

Dutchmen

George Hendrik Breitner
1857–1923
Two Amsterdam maids c. 1890
pastel 50 x 40 cm

Breitner, Two Amsterdam maids

George Breitner was a superb chron-icler of the tumultuous life of a large city. Van Gogh was not always com-plimentary about his work, once describing it as 'patches of faded colour on a piece of bleached, dusty and mouldy wallpaper.' He did like Breitner's portraits of women, though, and above all his 'ordinary women of the street.' That is the subject of this cursory pastel, which entered the collection of the Van Gogh Museum in 1990.

Jan Sluijters 1881–1957
Two women embracing,
'Femmes qui s'embrassent'
1906
oil on canvas 92 x 62,5 cm

One Dutch artist who quite clearly succumbed to Van Gogh's influence in his brushwork and use of colour was Jan Sluijters. He made this painting in Paris, where he lived for a while.
His teachers at the Rijksacademie in Amsterdam were pained by this painting, what they saw as 'a false attempt to capture the popular new colour moods and raw passion.' They condemned 'the foolhardy neglect of Beauty in the female forms, the quasi-brilliant but hurtful cruelty of colour, the coarse tech-nique mocking the material.' The Van Gogh Museum bought this painting in 1987.

Dutchmen

Sluijters, Two women embracing

Sculpture

Until recently, 19th-century sculpture played only a very modest part in the museum's presentation. The purchasing policy was focused almost exclusively on paintings, drawings and prints. That is now beginning to change. The main area of interest is French sculpture of the second half of the 19th century, with works ranging from the joyous decorative sculpture of Carpeaux to the realistic figures of Jules Dalou.

Carpeaux, Fisher-boy with a shell

Jean-Baptiste Carpeaux
1827–1875
Fisher-boy with a shell 1859
bronze h. 92 cm

Carpeaux's name is associated mainly with the decorative statues that he made for lavishly ornamented building projects in Paris. In 1865, his group *The dance* caused a scandal. It was intended for the new Opéra, but was considered too sensual and an offence against public morality; it was removed.
His Fisher-boy 94 attracted far less criticism, but then it was not erected on a street. It was exhibited several times at the Paris Salon from 1857 on, in various versions.
The theme of the simple fisher-boy was not new. Carpeaux's teachers, François Rude and Théodore Duret, had been making figures of this kind in the 1830s, when they were in great demand. Critics regarded them as a pretext for depicting a nude model: they were not truly realistic, nor were they academic. *The Gazette des Beaux-Arts* described Carpeaux's statue as follows: 'This little scamp, who is not nearly so naive as he pretends, wriggles like an ape with a stolen nut.'

Jules Dalou 1838–1902
'Grand paysan'
bronze 197 x 70 x 68 cm

This lifesize figure of a peasant who seems to be rolling up his shirtsleeves is one of the heroic figures that was intended to be part of a 'Monument au travail,' on which Dalou worked from 1889. The socially engaged artist made numerous studies for this group. He found his models on the street, in factories and in the countryside. Some of those sketches were later developed into monumental statues of workers.

Paul Gauguin 1848–1903
Vase 1886–1887
clay, partly glazed 14 x 12 x 9.5 cm

Gauguin took up ceramic design for
a while early on in his career. In
the autumn of 1886 he began experimenting with clay, and produced
more than 50 objects within six
months, among them this vase.
His ceramics were quite well
received, although it was doubted
that they would be a commercial
success. They were considered 'too
artistic.'
One side of this vase is decorated
with a semi-recumbent nude woman,
and the other with a tree and two
pigs rooting in the earth. It is known
from letters that the woman is
Cleopatra, the Egyptian ruler who
was regarded an archetypal *femme
fatale* in the 19th century. Pigs sym-
bolised lust.
There is an entry in a notebook stat-
ing that Gauguin gave this vase to
Theo van Gogh, possibly in gratitude
for his services as an art dealer.

Colophon

editors
Louis van Tilborgh, Fred Leeman,
Cor Krelekamp, Melchert Zwetsman

text
Annemiek Overbeek

text Story of a life
Louis van Tilborgh

translation
Michael Hoyle

design
Pieter Roozen , Amsterdam

layout
Monica Overdijk

cover photo
Luuk Kramer

lithography
Nederlof Repro, Cruquius Heemstede

printing
Waanders Drukkers, Zwolle

distribution
Waanders Uitgevers, Zwolle

The works illustrated in this guide belong to the
Vincent van Gogh Foundation with the excep-
tion of Paul Signac 76, Henri Harpignies 80,
Léon Lhermitte 82, Thomas Couture 84, Jules
Breton 85, Jean-François Raffaëlli 86, Felician
von Myrbach 87, Matthijs Maris 90, Fernand
Khnopff 90, François Aman-Jean 91, George
Breitner 92, Jan Sluijters 93, Jean-Baptiste
Carpeaux 94 en Jules Dalou 95, which are
owned by the Van Gogh Museum. The painting
by Claude Monet 74 is on loan from the
Netherlands Institute for Cultural Heritage,
Amsterdam.